Evaluative Studies

SECTIONS 235 AND 236

An economic evaluation of HUD's principal housing subsidy programs

Harrison G. Wehner, Jr.

SECTIONS 235 AND 236

An economic evaluation of HUD's principal housing subsidy programs

Harrison G. Wehner, Jr.

American Enterprise Institute for Public Policy Research
Washington D. C.

Harrison G. Wehner, Jr., is an economic consultant and lectures in economics at the Northern Virginia Regional Center of the University of Virginia.

Evaluative Studies 8, June 1973

ISBN 0-8447-3103-x

Library of Congress Catalog Card No. L.C. 73-83801

Printed in the United States of America

CONTENTS

I. INTRODUCTION

In the past two decades, the proportion of substandard housing in the United States has declined dramatically. In 1950, close to two-fifths of the nation's stock of dwelling units failed to meet minimum standards of structural soundness or facilities; by 1970 the ratio had fallen below 10 percent. Privately financed construction—some of it aided by government guarantees or insurance—was chiefly responsible for the striking improvement. The federal government had, it is true, promulgated numerous programs to improve the housing stock, both through new construction and the upgrading of existing units, and using both stimulus to the private market and direct intervention. But, at the same time that these efforts were responsible for the construction and rehabilitation of millions of units in the fifties and sixties, the government was responsible for destroying about the same number of units under its programs of slum clearance, highway building, and other public works.

Starting about 1970, however, federal programs began to make a net contribution to the nation's housing stock. The predominant source of that contribution has been subsidies to homeowners and tenants embodied, respectively, in Section 235 and Section 236 of the Housing and Urban Development Act of 1968. These programs, like the other housing efforts the government has undertaken, are aimed nominally at increasing the supply of standard housing for all the people and at providing the poor with adequate housing at prices they can afford.

The question this report addresses is whether the means that successive administrations have employed to achieve these aims are in fact the most efficient—in terms of sheer numbers and in terms of impact on one of the nation's single largest industries. Hardly

1

anyone quarrels with the desirability of improving housing generally or of ensuring decent homes for all regardless of income level. But common sense—as well as considerable analysis by investigators of all political-philosophical persuasions—suggests that neither objective requires the kind of direct subsidization of new construction that the Section 235 and 236 programs use.

Background to the Programs

Since the 1930s, the United States has sought to establish an effective national housing policy whose goal is decent housing and a suitable environment for lower-income persons. Early federal efforts were linked to urban renewal and consisted primarily of the construction of publicly financed and publicly administered housing. Critics have claimed that little was accomplished despite substantial expenditures of public funds. A recent report to the Congress by the comptroller general of the United States, for example, found that over the 1949-68 period the urban renewal program resulted in "a significant reduction in housing, especially for low- and moderate-income families, in project areas nationally."[1] What was left became more expensive as the supply decreased. Taking into account all federal housing programs, about as much housing used by the poor was destroyed in the fifties and sixties as was constructed in its place.

Criticism of this sort, and the growing concern in the 1960s over the shortage of adequate housing for families of modest incomes, led the Congress and President Johnson to commission two separate reviews of the housing problem. These reviews greatly influenced the drafting of the Housing and Urban Development Act of 1968.[2] In this act, Congress established major programs for housing subsidies, known by the section number of the National Housing Act of 1934, as amended, that embodied them: the Section 235 program of homeownership and the Section 236 program for multifamily rental housing. At the same time, Congress asked the President to establish a plan that would set forth annual goals for national housing production for the 1969-78 period.

The Section 235 homeownership program provides both mortgage insurance and cash payments for low- and moderate-income families to meet most of the mortgage interest cost on one- and two-family houses, old or new. The Section 236 program for multifamily rental housing also is aimed at reducing mortgage interest cost, and thus, in this case, rents.

The impact of these new subsidy programs has been substantial, as the accompanying table indicates. Subsidized housing starts for

2

lower-income households which over the 1961-68 period had averaged 3 to 5 percent of total housing production annually (including mobile home shipments and rehabilitation starts), jumped to 24 percent in 1970 and receded only slightly to 19 percent in 1971 (Table 1). During the 1969-71 period, the national housing production goals were easily achieved (Table 2). In part, it must be noted, the achievement was due to a rise in unsubsidized production—a rise that might have been even larger if resources had not been diverted into subsidized housing construction.

Purpose of This Study

Several reasons underlie the reexamination of housing subsidy programs undertaken here. First, the recent success of some of the programs and of private residential construction in general has brought the nation to the verge of a surplus of housing. This may be the time, therefore, for initiating a *gradual* phaseout of programs whose abrupt termination later, in the wake of soaring vacancies, foreclosures, and abandonments that they themselves would have helped to create, could gravely shock a troubled industry.

Second, the very success of the programs has raised the specter of enormous burdens on future federal budgets. The President stated in his 1971 report to Congress on housing goals that "present estimates suggest that the Federal Government will [by 1978] be paying out at least $7.5 billion annually in subsidies. Over the life of the mortgages this could amount to the staggering total of more than $200 billion." [3] A large share of this estimated cost would go to finance programs under Sections 235 and 236. Furthermore, the inefficiencies inherent in these programs—inefficiencies that are described in this report—make this amount more than double that which alternative means would absorb in achieving the same ends. Indeed, if the President's estimates are borne out, these programs will more than equal direct cash payments sufficient to lift the poor over the poverty line.

A third reason for reexamining these programs at this time is the alarming worsening of the inflation in construction costs. Though it is difficult to untangle this development from the inflation that afflicts the economy in general, ample evidence suggests that the subsidy programs have made no small contribution, and thus, perversely, have contributed to the disruption of the industry whose expansion and stabilization they were, in part, designed to enhance.

One source of this contribution lies in the provisions of the Davis-Bacon Act attached to the housing legislation. This act was

3

Table 1

U.S. HOUSING PRODUCTION, 1961-71

(in thousands of units, calendar years)

Type of Unit and Source	1961	1962	1963	1964	1965	1966	1967	1968	1969	1970	1971[a]
Subsidized Units [b]	39	42	51	59	70	82	105	195	229	471	482
New construction starts	36	39	48	55	64	72	91	167	200	435	445
Rehabilitation starts	3	3	3	4	6	10	14	28	29	41	37
Unsubsidized Units	1,419	1,572	1,745	1,697	1,662	1,341	1,470	1,696	1,713	1,435	1,998
New construction starts	1,329	1,454	1,594	1,506	1,446	1,124	1,230	1,378	1,300	1,034	1,638
Mobile home shipments	90	118	151	191	216	217	240	318	413	401	360
Total Production	1,458	1,614	1,796	1,756	1,732	1,423	1,575	1,891	1,942	1,906	2,480
New starts [c]	1,365	1,493	1,642	1,561	1,510	1,196	1,321	1,545	1,500	1,464	2,083

[a] Provisional

[b] Includes programs operated by the Department of Housing and Urban Development (Federal Housing Administration and low-rent public housing), the Veterans Administration, and the Department of Agriculture.

[c] Excluding rehabilitation starts and mobile home shipments.

Sources: Department of Housing and Urban Development, Division of Research and Statistics; Department of Commerce, Bureau of the Census, *Construction Reports*, Series C20.

Table 2

U.S. HOUSING GOALS, 1969-72

(in thousands of units, fiscal years)

Year and Item in Calculation	Total Production	Subsidized Units			Unsubsidized Units		
		Total	New construction	Rehabs	Total	New construction	Mobile homes
1969:							
Goal	2,001	198	155	43	1,803	1,440	363
Actual	1,997	192	163	29	1,806	1,437	369
% of goal achieved	100	97	105	67	100	100	102
1970:							
Goal	1,850	310	260	50	1,540	1,090	450
Actual	1,832	329	297	33	1,503	1,063	440
% of goal achieved	99	106	114	66	98	98	98
1971:							
Goal	2,040	505	445	60	1,535	1,060	475
Actual	2,276	480	439	41	1,796	1,359	437
% of goal achieved	112	95	98	68	117	128	92
1972:							
Goal	2,330	650	575	75	1,680	1,230	450
Actual [a]	2,799	469	420	49	2,330	1,780	550
% of goal achieved	120	72	73	65	139	145	122

[a] Estimated by HUD.

Source: *Third Annual Report on National Housing Goals*, Message from the President to Congress (Washington, D.C.: U.S. Government Printing Office, 1971), Table 1, pp. 4-5; and data supplied by HUD, office of the secretary.

designed to protect local construction workers building federally sponsored projects from the competition of nonlocal laborers. In some instances, however, it forces contractors building subsidized housing to pay rates above the going market, thereby increasing the cost of HUD's projects and working at cross-purposes with the nation's housing goals.

Fourth, concern has also been aroused by the extent to which programs relying almost exclusively on new construction have fostered the decay and abandonment of existing structures that, with adequate maintenance, could have filled some of the nation's housing needs.

Fifth, despite their apparent success, many questions have been raised about the administration of these programs. A recent congressional investigation found instances of fraud and exploitation, especially in the Section 235 rehabilitation program.[4] In fact, the program is an open invitation to fraud. No matter what the price of the house (within certain limits),[5] the purchaser's monthly payments are limited to 20 percent of his adjusted income, and the government pays the balance. The purchaser, therefore, has little or no incentive to negotiate on price. And the seller, for his part, has a powerful incentive to induce a buyer, by various devices including the gift of the down payment, to pay an above-market price. These problems have primarily afflicted existing-house transactions; given the current level of building costs, statutory ceilings on mortgages leave little room to construct housing whose value is less than its HUD-appraised value.

Defaults on mortgages insured and subsidized under Section 235 (primarily rehabilitated housing) have made the federal government the nation's largest slumlord, with over 50,000 homes in its possession. This consequence is hardly surprising since an eligible family may pay less each month for a house that it nominally purchases than it would pay in rent. With no stake to lose, the family will abandon its "purchase" as readily as it will move from a rented unit. The competition from subsidized housing is also believed to be a factor in the extensive decay and abandonment of existing rental housing.

Finally, thoughtful observers have increasingly questioned the fairness of programs that serve some of the poor but not others, and that ask middle-income taxpayers to support housing for the poor that is sometimes better than their own.

In face of such criticism, defenders of the subsidy programs argue that they permit the nation to meet its annual housing production goals at costs that are not excessive, and that the problems they pose can be solved with more operating experience and better administrative adjustments.[6]

The divergence of opinion over the programs arises from (1) the complexity of the subsidy mechanism, (2) the evolution of the programs as the Congress has sought to establish a national housing policy, and (3) the technical difficulties of measuring the impact of subsidies generally on the distribution of income and allocation of resources in the economy. Added to this are the differing criteria, based on differing goals, that are applied in assaying the programs: some see them as means of increasing the total supply of housing, others as devices for decreasing the cost of housing to beneficiaries or for redistributing income in favor of the poor.

It may be that the private and public benefits these subsidies afford in increased output, better allocation of resources, and redistribution of income indeed outweigh their burden on the taxpayers and on the economy generally. But the magnitude of their benefits is not known. Nor are their costs, for assessment is also complicated by a mixture of incentives whose costs are not regularly measured. The Section 235 and 236 programs encompass a number of financial incentives, some of which are not subject to annual budget review. As a further complication, the incentives take both direct and indirect forms: the first involves cash payments to mortgage lenders on behalf of qualifying homeowners or tenants, in order to reduce the interest rate on mortgage loans insured by HUD and to absorb discount points charged by lenders when market interest rates are above HUD ceilings. And the second involves tax preferences to investors in Section 236 projects to encourage a greater flow of risk capital into this market.

Even without definitive answers to these questions about the costs and benefits of the subsidy programs, and even with all their problems, they are one means of meeting the nation's housing goals. The alternative may be not the abandonment of these programs, but their integration into a scheme of devices that would spur both new construction and an optimal amount of rehabilitation and maintenance of existing structures. Such a program would allow policy makers—and the nation—to meet the need for decent housing at reasonable cost. It would do so economically and without undue disruption of stable urban neighborhoods or offense to the nation's sense of equity.

7

II. PRINCIPAL HOUSING SUBSIDIES

In establishing housing subsidy programs, Congress has stated its intent only in general terms and without a detailed description of the expected results. These programs have been justified not on specific economic grounds, but rather by the notion that they would benefit disadvantaged members of society.[1]

Legislative Background

Ostensibly, subsidy programs have been created by Congress to increase employment, encourage housing production, and provide decent housing for lower-income families. The effects on output have not been specifically introduced into the argument, although the benefits of decent housing in terms of improved neighborhoods and social conditions have been implicit in it. No clear rationale has been set forth for using housing subsidies to redistribute income in favor of the poor. It may be noted that the programs established in past years have provided capital subsidies to encourage production of new housing units; and little has been said about subsidizing the operation of existing housing units that can provide the same flow of services to beneficiaries.[2]

The evolution of a national housing policy in the United States started with the depression and the wave of mortgage foreclosures in the early 1930s.[3] The Federal Home Loan Bank system and the Home Owners Loan Corporation were established to provide sources of liquidity to savings and loan associations and liberal mortgage terms to homeowners. The Federal Housing Administration was established in 1934 to insure residential mortgages. All these steps were basically antidepression measures aimed at encouraging home-ownership, reviving home building, and creating employment. They embodied relatively small subsidy elements—in the case of FHA mortgage insurance, none at all.[4]

The first effort made to assist poor families directly was the low-rent public housing program enacted in 1937. Its basic intent was to provide eligible households with new and inexpensive units, to upgrade neighborhoods,[5] and to stimulate employment.

The Housing Act of 1949 provided the first clear definition of a national housing policy: "the realization as soon as feasible of the goal of a decent home and suitable living environment for every American family." The act expanded the slum clearance provisions of the 1937 legislation by providing a program of urban renewal with subsidies to help finance nearly a million units of public housing. The aim was to contribute "to the development and redevelopment of communities and to the advancement of the growth, wealth, and security of the nation," and the subsidies were to be directed toward "families with income so low that they are not being decently housed in new or existing units. . . ."[6] The terms of the legislation implied a desire to foster positive externalities by upgrading neighborhoods, as well as to redistribute income toward the poor. The act also initiated a home loan program on favorable terms for farm housing, to be administered by the Farmers Home Administration.

The Housing Act of 1950 provided direct loans at low interest rates for college housing,[7] and expanded the Veterans Administration housing program established during World War II. The VA program entailed an element of subsidy to encourage production, but the measure was not intended to be of long duration, nor to serve low- and moderate-income households exclusively.

The first FHA program of direct loans for rental units that bore interest rates below the market level was established in 1959, and was known as the Section 202 program of housing for the elderly. The concept was extended to all moderate-income households in 1961 under Section 221(d)(3).

A private counterpart of public low-rent housing was established in 1965 under the rent supplement program authorizing federal payments on behalf of low-income tenants for rentals in privately financed and owned projects. Only nonprofit, cooperative, or limited-dividend groups are eligible to receive funds from the government on behalf of qualified tenants. In 1971, the typical tenant had an income of $2,185, paid $51 rent, and received a monthly subsidy of $86. A limited subsidy to encourage homeownership for low-income households was introduced in 1966.

As part of its reaffirmation of the national housing policy statement of 1949, the Housing and Urban Development Act of 1968 called for the production of 26 million new housing units over the 1969-78 decade. Six million of these were to be subsidized for low- and moderate-income households; and to implement this part of the program, the act contained two new programs, operating under Section 235 (homeownership units) and Section 236 (multifamily rental housing).

In order to reduce the immediate impact on the current federal budget, the new programs avoid the use of direct long-term federal loans, and rely instead on mortgage insurance and on subsidies on part of the interest on eligible mortgages; these subsidies are higher than those under Section 202 or 221(d)(3). The mortgages are originated by private lenders, who may retain them in their portfolios or sell them to the Federal National Mortgage Association.

More recently, Congress augmented subsidies for public housing to cover spiraling operating and maintenance costs. Also, it established a limited subsidy program for middle-income housing and authorized an experimental housing allowance program, now underway in Kansas City and slated for other test cities.[8]

Description of Housing Subsidy Programs

The federal housing subsidy programs are intended to reduce the private capital cost of producing new or substantially rehabilitated housing units. As a direct approach HUD pays cash to lenders in order to reduce the cost of debt service to the homeowners and tenants. Indirectly, investors in low-income housing also receive tax preferences in the form of favorable depreciation allowances; and the federal government provides the equivalent of an additional capital subsidy by guaranteeing the mortgage on low-income and public housing projects, thus in effect reducing lenders' risks and thereby lowering interest rates. These guaranteed mortgages, however, make it more difficult than it otherwise would be for other borrowers to raise funds at favorable rates. Except for recent changes in the public housing program and the new experimental program of housing allowances, no attempt has been made to subsidize operating and maintenance costs of existing units.

The federal housing subsidy programs can be categorized according to the nature of ownership and the locus of decision making.[9] Subsidized housing units developed under programs administered by the Department of Housing and Urban Development and by the Department of Agriculture are privately financed and owned. HUD and USDA provide mortgage insurance for these units, and pay cash subsidies to reduce the effective interest cost of the debt.

The public housing program is administered and controlled by local housing authorities under the direction of HUD. HUD makes annual contributions to local housing authorities to help meet debt service payments on local bonds issued to finance construction, as well as special payments to the elderly and handicapped living in public housing. In recent years it has made payments to local authorities to cover a portion of their operating and maintenance expenses.[10]

In 1971, the HUD and USDA programs accounted for 82 percent of federally subsidized housing production, including rehabilitation units; the public housing program provided the remaining 18 percent. The subsidy programs administered by the two departments include the activity under Sections 202, 221(d)(3), 235, and 236. Of these, the last two, which are the subject of this paper, are by far the most important. Their share in total subsidized production has increased, while the older programs, carried out under Sections 202 and 221(d)(3), have been gradually phased out. In 1971, units started under Sections 235 and 236 accounted for 80 percent of privately financed subsidized production and 66 percent of federally subsidized housing production including public housing.

Subsidies under Sections 235 and 236

Cash Subsidies. The interest rate subsidy provided for in Sections 235 and 236 is based on the difference between monthly mortgage payments (or the equivalent "market rent") amortized at market interest rates and (1) mortgage payments amortized at 1 percent, or (2) payments equal to 25 percent of monthly adjusted income of tenants (20 percent in the homeownership program), whichever is the smaller amount.

To be eligible for a subsidy under Section 235, a buyer must have an adjusted income—defined as total family income minus earnings of minor children minus 5 percent minus $300 per minor child—no higher than 135 percent of the local limit for admission to public housing. The required down payment is $200 (including closing costs). In 1971 the typical Section 235 family paid $91 a month and the government paid the mortgagor $81 a month subsidy.

The Section 236 subsidy is paid to the project owner, and the regulations are similar to those on Section 235. In 1971, the typical 236 family paid $115 rent, while the government provided a subsidy of $75 a month.

12

The economic intent of the interest rate subsidy was not explicitly spelled out by the Congress in the Housing Act of 1968 or in earlier legislation. Although it tends to raise interest rates in general by increasing the demand for loans, the subsidy does not directly increase the financial return to lenders of mortgage funds. Rather, it reduces the cost of providing housing services from new construction. The subsidy should therefore be considered a device to lower consumer prices, the chief benefit of which is a redistribution of income in favor of low-income households. Administratively, the subsidy is directed mainly at consumers of housing: HUD makes interest payments to lenders on behalf of homeowners and tenants. The actual reduction in unit prices and expansion in output is determined by the relevant elasticities of supply and demand.

Subsidy payments are also made to curtail discounts on HUD-insured mortgages during periods when market interest rates rise above the ceilings established by HUD. This subsidy was created during the tight money period of 1969 when the President, under the special assistance authority of Section 301 of the National Housing Act, authorized the Government National Mortgage Association (GNMA) to purchase, at or near par, mortgages on housing constructed under the HUD programs that contain interest rate subsidies. Instead of holding these mortgages, the total value of which would show up as an expenditure in the federal budget, GNMA subsequently sells them to the Federal National Mortgage Association (FNMA) at discounts reflecting the market rate of interest. GNMA thereby absorbs the discount that would otherwise be borne by the builder/developer of FHA-insured subsidized housing. This program is known as the Tandem Plan.

The purpose of this subsidy is to expand low-income housing production by making returns on investment under the HUD subsidy programs competitive with returns on conventionally financed construction. The subsidy is therefore a consumer-use subsidy (benefitting consumers primarily through output effects) directed mainly at producers: it is designed to circumvent the HUD-imposed interest rate ceilings.

Tax Subsidies. Low-income housing projects insured by HUD under Sections 221(d)(3) and 236 of the National Housing Act (or similar state and local statutes) are the subject of tax benefits beyond those afforded all new residential property.[11] Under the 1969 Tax Reform Act, Congress permitted continued application of accelerated depreciation (double-declining-balance or sum-of-the-years-digits methods) to all new residential property. But for investors in low-income

13

housing it also provided (1) favorable capital gains treatment of sales proceeds representing the excess of accelerated over straight-line depreciation and (2) generous roll-over provisions.

Normally, when depreciable property is sold, the excess of permitted accelerated over straight-line depreciation is taxed as ordinary income in the following way: For new residential property, the recapture rate is 100 percent for the first 100 months; after that, the rate drops by 1 percent per month, until, at the end of $16\frac{2}{3}$ years (200 months), only the capital gains rates apply. For investors in low-income housing, the 1969 Tax Reform Act provided for a reduction in the holding time with full recapture to 20 months. After 10 years (120 months) there is no recapture and all gain is taxed at the capital gains rate. Insofar as (1) accelerated depreciation allowances exceed "true" depreciation and (2) straight-line depreciation allowances do not fall short of "true" depreciation, the lower capital gains tax rate on the excess of accelerated over straight-line depreciation, included in the sales proceeds, may be viewed as a subsidy.

The second tax subsidy unique to investors in low-income housing is the indefinite deferral of capital gains taxes and the avoidance of recapture of sales proceeds representing "excess" depreciation when a project is sold at a profit to tenants, or to a nonprofit organization of tenants, and the proceeds are reinvested in another low-income project. This provision encourages such sales after the first few years of ownership, during which time both depreciation benefits and annual returns on equity are at their peaks.

These tax preferences have a direct impact on investors but are intended, through their indirect effects, to function as consumer-use subsidies. Their objective is to make capital resources available for production of low-income housing at costs competitive with alternative investments of comparable risk. This justification is similar to the arguments for the Tandem Plan.

Some state and local governments provide an additional tax subsidy by exempting low-income housing from real property taxes. The aim is to subsidize such households through reductions in monthly rents.

The Offsetting Effect of the Davis-Bacon Act

The cash subsidies and tax benefits, which are directly or indirectly designed to benefit consumers of housing services, are partially offset by the provisions of the Davis-Bacon Act of 1931.[12] This act, which is incorporated in the National Housing Act, requires the Department of Labor to determine "prevailing" wages and fringe benefits, which then become the minimum standards for workers on federally funded or sponsored projects. The purpose is to protect local laborers on federal construction, or federally sponsored construction, from the competition of low-wage nonlocal labor. Consequently, contractors building HUD-insured subsidized or nonsubsidized multifamily housing projects are required by law to pay these "prevailing" wages, although the act is not applicable to home mortgages and consequently does not affect the Section 235 program.

Studies of the impact of the Davis-Bacon Act on the construction industry indicate that "prevailing" wages—as determined by the Department of Labor—have often been higher than actual market wages for local labor.[13] In such instances the cost of labor to builders of federally sponsored projects rises, for workers can be engaged only at premium prices. This means higher subsidies,[14] if contractors or tenants are not to absorb this cost. The regulatory provisions of the Davis-Bacon Act frequently have the effect of diverting subsidies into the overpayment of construction workers and away from the provision of more housing.

III. THE CONCEPT OF HOUSING SUBSIDIES

A subsidy is a negative tax: it lowers prices to the recipient of an economic good and thus changes output, according to the supply and demand elasticities. A subsidy is a transfer payment disbursed directly by government to consumers, producers, or providers of factors of production. It influences private market behavior through a tie to the buying and selling of specific goods or services. It does not require an equivalent compensation from recipients, although the government's objective is to elicit a specific response from them. It modifies market activity by changing market prices rather than by supplanting the private market with government control.

A subsidy is distinguished from cash welfare payments in that it calls for a specific economic response before it is paid. It differs also from the direct provision of public services (such as highways or schooling), for which no private market exists.

Subsidies have been used throughout the history of the United States as tools of public policy to achieve specific economic objectives. A recent congressional study estimated that the current gross budgetary cost of federal subsidy programs amounted to $63 billion in fiscal year 1970. Housing subsidies (including $5.4 billion in mortgage interest and in property tax deductions from taxable personal income) accounted for $8.4 billion of the total.[1]

The same study found that federal subsidies constitute a diverse and pervasive system of economic assistance, largely hidden from public scrutiny and generally not well coordinated or controlled by federal executive agencies. Moreover, the objectives of these programs were found to be poorly defined and their impacts on markets little understood.

Economic Objectives of Subsidies

One objective of a subsidy scheme is to alter the composition of economic activity, through changes in the relative prices of subsidized and unsubsidized goods and services. Among the economic justifications offered for subsidies are (1) the assumed inability of producers and consumers operating in factor and product markets to bring about an optimal allocation of resources, and (2) the price rigidities caused by regulatory authority, by legislative enactments, and by market power, that distort resource allocation. The argument holds that these inefficiencies may be severe enough in some cases that government intervention can make some persons better off without making others worse off.

Legislative enactment and executive regulation have created market imperfections in the housing sector. Such measures as control over interest rates that financial institutions may pay or charge and statutory ceilings on the rates on FHA-VA and other mortgages have had the effect of curtailing the flow of funds to mortgage markets when interest rates rise.[2] Restrictive work rules and limitations on training programs imposed by unions, archaic building codes, and restrictive zoning ordinances also impede the free operation of the market.

Externalities—spill-over costs and benefits—also may prevent a market from valuing an economic activity properly.[3] If, for example, owing to so-called neighborhood effects, the social benefits of expenditures for home improvements are greater than the private benefits to the property owner, the allocation of resources resulting from individual decisions might be suboptimal because they were based on private costs and benefits.

A government bounty paid to citizens who turn in their firearms exemplifies another justification for subsidies—the desire to alter the scope of certain activities. The assumption here is that fewer citizens should own firearms; and there is no need, beyond the bounty itself, to compensate either party if those financing the bounty believe they will be better off if no firearms are held by private citizens and those turning in their guns find the bounty adequate incentive to do so.

Subsidies have also been justified as a mechanism to redistribute income. Total economic output may be considered improperly allocated if the market distribution of goods and services does not accord with society's ethical values. The food stamp program administered by the U.S. Department of Agriculture is an example of this use of a subsidy. But subsidies for this purpose are difficult to

18

justify because they make some persons better off only at the expense of others—unless those who finance them believe themselves better off because others benefit. But, however the costs and benefits are distributed, subsidies obtainable only by specific varieties of consumption distort choices and are less efficient than direct money grants.[4]

Measuring Benefits

The effect of a subsidy depends upon the relative supply and demand elasticities of the good or service to which the subsidy is directed. Benefits can be categorized according to whether the subsidy is aimed at (1) reducing inefficiencies brought about by market imperfections, (2) helping to internalize losses or gains from an activity, (3) changing the scope of an activity deemed important, or (4) accomplishing a "better" distribution of income.

The real income benefits are shared among consumers, producers, and other factors of production according to the price incidence of the subsidy as determined by the relevant elasticities of supply and demand. A subsidy to sellers of a product (causing a shift in the supply curve to the right—that is, causing sellers to offer more goods at a given price) will reduce its market price. A subsidy paid to the purchaser of a product (causing a shift in the demand curve to the right—that is, causing purchasers to demand more at a given price) will raise market prices. In neither case does the change in price fully match the subsidy. In the first, the seller must share the benefits of the subsidy with the consumer, who will buy the increased output only because of the lower price. In the second, the consumer must share the benefits of the subsidy he receives with the seller, who will provide the increased output only because of the higher price.

The benefits of a subsidy paid to factors of production—such as an interest rate subsidy to lenders of risk capital—are not limited to those to whom it is paid. With competitive conditions in capital markets, such a subsidy reduces interest rates but not by the full amount of the subsidy because more capital will be supplied only at higher prices. This situation might be considered a special example of a subsidy to the sellers of a product—in this case, money. To the extent that the subsidy is meant to channel capital to a particular use, it diverts it from others.[5] Moreover, the borrower (builder) may not be able to retain as profit that part of the subsidy passed on to him in the form of reduced interest rates because he may have to reduce the rent of the housing.

Output effects measure the ability of a subsidy to reallocate resources in the economy. They are greatest when supply and demand elasticities with respect to price are relatively high. If market imperfections have hindered the price system in allocating resources efficiently, then subsidies that change the level of output may divert resources to better uses.

A difficult measurement problem arises in determining whether resources are in fact being diverted to more efficient uses or the losses in the sectors of the economy (or industry) from which they are shifted exceed the gains in the subsidized sector. When a subsidy stimulates output of one kind of good or service at the expense of depressing output elsewhere, it must be defended on the basis that the former is preferred over the latter.

The legislative intent of a subsidy may therefore not always be realized. A direct cash housing allowance paid to low-income families, for example, could lead primarily to higher prices for housing and higher incomes for its factors of production if the supplies are inelastic with respect to price.[6] Such a scheme could simply give low-income families the means to compete with others for the existing housing stock, and to displace them, without adding appreciably to the stock, at least in the short run. A study by Richard Muth, however, has found that for every 1 percent increase in income, the number of substandard housing units occupied falls by 3.3 percent.[7]

Evaluating Costs and Benefits

Conceptually, subsidies can be evaluated within a cost-benefit framework. If the subsidy improves efficiency, those who gain could compensate those who lose and still be better off than they were before. The evaluation of the subsidy could, therefore, be based on whether the net gain offsets the real resource costs. Ideally, the amount of subsidy should be fixed so that at the margin net gain equals real resource costs. An increase in subsidy payments beyond the margin would impose real resource costs greater than the net gain and thus cause a net loss. The economy can have too much of a good thing, whether it be vocational rehabilitation, medical care, or housing.

Realistically, the impact a subsidy program has on the level of efficiency in the economy is almost impossible to quantify. Nevertheless, it can be said that an inept program exacerbates existing market imperfections or introduces distortions where none existed. Under such circumstances, a gross loss occurs in the form of an overall reduction in economic efficiency as well as a loss to those who finance the subsidy.

It is almost as difficult to quantify the impact of a subsidy program on the distribution of income. This effect can be estimated only by a review of the adjustment process as resource allocation shifts from the initial to the new equilibrium value of output. Such an evaluation cannot be purely quantitative. It must rest on how the subsidy program distributes its income benefits and whether this distribution fulfills the intent of Congress.

IV. WHO BENEFITS?
WHO PAYS—AND HOW MUCH?

In this section, an attempt is made to quantify the benefits of the programs that HUD administers under Sections 235 and 236 of the Housing and Urban Development Act of 1968. The price effects of individual subsidy devices are discussed and the subsidies are then aggregated for an examination of output effects.

Price Effects

Cash Subsidies. One way to estimate real income benefits from the interest subsidy (determined by the impact it has on prices) is to compute the difference between (1) payments for principal and interest (or rent equivalent) by occupants of subsidized housing, and (2) payments for principal and interest (adjusted for equity accumulation in case of owner-occupied units) by occupants of comparable nonsubsidized housing.[1] This procedure helps determine whether subsidized housing is more expensive to build than nonsubsidized housing of comparable quality. It assumes a completely elastic supply of housing; otherwise, the greater demand for housing stimulated by the subsidy would raise housing prices generally—to a degree that would depend on the elasticity of supply. Thus, while households receiving the subsidy would pay less than nonsubsidized households for comparable housing, all housing would cost more than it did at the initial equilibrium. This problem can be dealt with by estimating first the actual payments subsidized households make for housing services against the full cost of comparable housing, and then the industry-wide price impact of the subsidy.

Henry Schechter has estimated the distribution of cash subsidy benefits by comparing, on a nationwide basis, data on owner-occupied and rental housing insured, respectively, under the Section 203 and 207 nonsubsidized programs, with data on Section 235 and 236 housing. He found that homeowners derive 97 to 98 percent of the subsidy benefits, and the balance accrues to builders, who can obtain higher profits under the Section 235 program—partly because homes financed by these mortgages sell faster than others and financing costs for the builder are correspondingly reduced.

Schechter found that land prices per square foot for Section 235 homes were significantly lower than those for Section 203 homes. He attributed this difference to the statutory mortgage limitations on the Section 235 program, which have encouraged construction of Section 235 homes in outlying suburban areas where land is comparatively cheap. Whether sellers profit more from the sale of such land for Section 235 housing rather than for Section 203 housing cannot be determined from the data.

Available data suggest that tenants in Section 236 units receive the full share of the cash (interest rate) subsidies disbursed by HUD, if it is assumed that the increased demand for funds does not raise interest rates generally. The contractual assistance payment per unit in Section 236 projects for which HUD mortgage insurance commitments were made was approximately $75 per month from fiscal 1969 through fiscal 1971. Since the difference between the median rents for a Section 207 unit ($227) and for a Section 236 unit ($139) was $88, the monthly median rent plus subsidy on Section 236 units was somewhat lower than the rent on comparable nonsubsidized Section 207 units.[3]

The reallocation process involved in shifting labor and building materials to production of subsidized housing has certainly contributed to the sharp rise in residential building costs in recent years. As measured by the Boeckh indexes, the quarterly rise in costs of residential construction was generally less steep than that for nonresidential construction during the 1969-70 period. With the increase in housing starts in the second quarter of 1970, building costs in general began to rise. However, the rate of increase in costs of nonresidential building leveled off beginning in 1971, while residential construction costs continued to move upward sharply, moderating only when the rate of increase in overall inflation abated. Considering that subsidized housing production was the principal source of expansion in the residential construction market in 1970 (when it accounted for 32 percent of total new starts), and that the subsidy programs continued to absorb a large share of resources throughout 1971-72, a significant industry-wide price effect can reasonably be attributed to the program. Making a rough approximation, Schechter estimated that residential building costs rose by 2.5 percent in 1971 on account of the subsidy program.[4]

The available data suggest that the major share of benefits from cash subsidies has been distributed to eligible housing consumers. But the benefit has been eroded by the general increase in prices in the industry caused by the added demand for housing induced by subsidy payments. Buyers of nonsubsidized housing have therefore suffered a loss.

Tax Subsidies. As noted in Section II, all newly constructed rental housing qualifies for accelerated depreciation allowances. Such allowances increase the return on equity for those who are able to offset these deductions against other current income. The subsidy, if any, involved in accelerated depreciation is available to all owners of new rental housing and therefore cannot be considered a special benefit for owners of Section 236 housing.

The tax preferences reserved exclusively for investors in low-income rental housing projects in the form of favorable capital gains treatment and roll-over provisions were also explained above. An investor in a 50 percent tax bracket who sells his interest in a Section 236 project to a qualifying tenant organization after four or five years and reinvests the proceeds in another low-income project could receive the full tax benefits available. Over the four- to five-year period, these provisions might mean an annual return 6 to 7 percent higher than that on a comparable nonsubsidized project.[5] To qualify for these benefits, however, the sale must be to tenants or a tenant organization. This theoretical added return on investment in a Section 236 project may not be easy to realize in practice, because it is not always possible to sell the project at the appropriate time to the appropriate buyer.

Whether higher possible returns on investment in low-income housing reflect greater risk or simply a more lucrative investment is hard to determine—if, indeed, the problem can be stated in these terms at all. Investors must consider other factors in deciding whether to invest in a Section 236 project or in a HUD-insured nonsubsidized project. For one thing, rents for eligible tenants are lower in the subsidized projects than in comparable dwellings in the open market, and vacancy rates may therefore be lower, thus cutting the potential drain on profits. On the other hand, investors in nonsubsidized projects can earn a higher annual return on their equity than the 6 percent statutory limit for subsidized projects, and they may have lower maintenance and operating costs. In both subsidized and nonsubsidized projects, HUD will insure mortgages up to 90 percent of replacement value, so that investors' leverage (equity-to-replacement ratio) is the same in both cases. Higher return on subsidized housing does not necessarily indicate the presence of "excess" profits. It could also reflect greater risk or lower cash flow.[6]

This discussion suggests how difficult it is to determine how much of the additional return to investors represents the premium required to attract equity capital into low-income housing. It is clear, however, that existing financial incentives have stimulated the flow of equity capital for low-income housing, judging by the increase in production in recent years.

Are these special incentives excessive? If investors operating in the open markets for HUD-insured multifamily housing projects are willing to pay a premium for equity interests originated by developers, the reason would seem to be that they find the return on investment owing to the special tax provisions sufficiently high to warrant doing so. In this case, it appears that the tax benefits for investors are passed on to the developer.

This point requires a brief discussion of the mechanics of financing HUD multifamily housing projects. The equity interest a developer has in a low-income multifamily housing project generally amounts to 10 percent of total project replacement cost inasmuch as HUD provides mortgage insurance up to 90 percent of replacement costs. Developers normally organize limited partnerships so that the tax deductions generated by the project can be "passed through" to investors. (Nonprofit sponsors, who receive 100 percent HUD mortgage insurance, are not considered here because they do not have taxable income to shelter.) HUD allows the required 10 percent equity to be met by the developer and his builder out of fixed allowances for builder-sponsor profit and risk, builder overhead allowances, and legal and organizational fees. These allowances and fees are designed to provide a reasonable return to the developer and builder, given the risk, effort, and time involved in carrying out a Section 236 project.

Because developers often prefer cash over tax benefits, they generally sell all or part of their equity interest to investors, who become limited partners. The par value of this equity is 11.11 percent of the mortgage (the 10 percent equity divided by the 90 percent mortgage). Any excess over par value paid to the developer by investors may be considered an additional profit. But it is nearly impossible to identify the portion of this premium that reflects the value of the special tax benefits generated by the low-income housing project, because (1) the fees HUD sets may not in fact reflect alternative opportunities for builders and developers, (2) the equity of a well-designed project having an unusual location may command premium prices, and (3) investors may be attracted by a project in which they have limited financial liability in case of operating losses, or are required to put up less cash at the earlier stages of development—that is, a project of lower investor risk.

The difficulty of untangling the effects of these various factors is seen in Table 3, which summarizes the prices paid syndicates of limited-partner investors for equity interests in 20 HUD-insured housing projects for low- and moderate-income families located throughout the United States. These data give no clear indication that the premium paid to developers is necessarily greater for subsidized than for nonsubsidized projects. Too many elements intrude in the effort to judge how investors establish expected rates of return. The favorable capital gains treatment and roll-over provisions available to investors in subsidized housing form only one of these elements, and might indeed be swamped by the accelerated depreciation allowances available to both subsidized and nonsubsidized projects.

The Effect of Davis-Bacon Requirements on Subsidies. According to the General Accounting Office, over the 1962-70 period construction costs on federally sponsored projects were raised by 5-15 percent because the "prevailing wages" that the Department of Labor established under the provisions of the Davis-Bacon Act were above actual market wages.[7]

Table 3
PURCHASE PRICES OF EQUITIES IN HUD-INSURED MULTIFAMILY HOUSING PROJECTS

Nature of HUD-Insured Project	Range of Purchase Prices [a] (percent)
Subsidized	
236 program	11.95–15.24
221(d)(3) rent supplement program	14.98–15.99
Nonsubsidized	
221(d)(4) program	13.88–14.73

[a] Expressed as percent of mortgage value insured by HUD.
Source: E. F. Hutton and Company, Inc., *American Housing Partners—II,* a prospectus published June 29, 1972.

Table 4

IMPACT OF DAVIS-BACON ACT ON HOUSING COSTS [a]

Trade Item	Job Cost	Labor Content	Davis-Bacon Wage/hr.	Non-Union Wage/hr.	Wage Cost Excesses
Concrete	$ 84,690	68%	$7.70	$4.50	$23,733
Masonry	189,885	74	8.40	7.15	20,910
Metals	16,800	40	8.55	7.70	668
Carpentry	203,112	33	7.85	5.00	24,335
Waterproofing ⎫ Roofing Sheet metal Insulation ⎭	32,123	50	6.60	5.75	2,069
Drywall	47,050	47	7.85	5.50	6,620
Ceramic tile	8,164	55	7.55	6.50	624
Wood flooring	29,918	47	7.55	6.50	1,956
Painting	37,680	68	7.25	6.20	3,711
Plumbing ⎫ HVAC ⎭	133,485	34	9.15	7.50	8,184
Electrical	54,963	31	8.75	7.40	2,629
Total	837,870	—	—	—	95,639
				Net Difference	11.4%

a Based on cost estimates made in 1971 for a 61-unit Section 236 project in Washington, D. C.

Source: Information obtained from computer records of Construction Assurance Consultants, Inc., McGraw-Hill and Dodge publications, and the Departments of Labor and Commerce.

The data given in Table 4 suggest that the cost of a typical low-income housing project built in the Washington, D. C. area in 1971 may have been some 11 percent higher as a result of the differences between "prevailing wage determinations" and normal wages for local workers on residential structures. The cost comparison in Table 4 is based on nonunion rates, rather than on some weighted average of actual market wages for all workers by job classification, and may overstate the difference.

In urban areas such as the District of Columbia, where most workers are unionized, the cost premium imposed by the manner in which the Davis-Bacon Act is administered may be lower than it is in suburban areas where nonunion workers form a greater share of the labor force. Because most low-income multifamily housing under federal sponsorship has been built in urban areas, the level of regulatory subsidy to construction labor imposed by the Davis-Bacon Act may have been relatively low. As more low-income housing is built in suburban areas, where contractors are able to employ more nonunion labor, the size of the subsidy to construction workers will increase.

Output Effects

The figures shown in Table 1 indicate that the subsidy programs established under the Housing and Urban Development Act of 1968 have encouraged the output of subsidized units. But did this increase stem from a more efficient use of available resources or was it simply a shift of resources from other housing markets or from other sectors of the economy?

In an effort to ascertain whether the increase in production that began in late 1968 was brought about by the Section 235-236 subsidies, the SSRC-MIT-PENN-Econometric model for the U.S. housing industry was used to generate forecasts of housing starts for the 1969-71 period. In the model, the determinants of housing demand are assumed to be real permanent income per capita, the implicit rental price for the stock of housing relative to general consumer prices, and the cost of mortgage money. Housing supply is determined by builders' responses to housing prices and construction costs; and demand shifts with the relation between cost of capital and the ratio of implicit rental prices to housing prices, rising when the first drops relative to the second. The bidding up of housing prices relative to construction costs increases production.[8] Since the model was not altered in 1968 to take the new housing subsidy programs into account, a discrepancy between actual and estimated starts could have been expected starting in 1969, unless the expansion of subsidized production occurred at the expense of construction in other housing markets.

On the basis of the model's estimates for the 1969-71 period, there is some indication that the expansion in subsidized housing production (primarily under the Section 235 and 236 programs) beginning in late 1968 constituted an actual net increase in total housing production rather than a mere substitution of production within housing markets—though substitution may also have taken place. Over the 1958-68 period, the model estimated actual housing starts with an average annual error of 5.7 percent; over the 1969-71 period, the model underestimated actual starts by an average of 16.8 percent. The size of the error increased along with subsidized housing production during this period. When the model was adjusted to take into account the value of subsidized housing starts, the annual error was reduced to 1.3 percent (see Table 5).

One explanation for the underestimate of starts lies in the role the cost of mortgage money plays in the determination of demand. This factor has little impact on the demand for subsidized housing because higher mortgage costs (that is, interest costs) are offset by higher subsidy payments, leaving unaffected the demand of those eligible for subsidized housing.

Table 5

ANALYSIS OF THE SSRC-MIT-PENN HOUSING SECTOR MODEL AND SUBSIDIZED HOUSING STARTS
(in millions of current dollars)

Year and Quarter	Actual Total Housing Starts [a] (1)	Model Error (2)	Subsidized Starts [b] (3)	Model Error as % of Actual Starts (4) = (2) ÷ (1)	Model Error Corrected by Subsidized Starts as % of Actual Starts (5) = (3) − (2) ÷ (1)
1969 (1)	6,296	426	385	6.76	− .65
(2)	5,864	213	506	3.63	4.99
(3)	5,592	311	590	5.56	4.98
(4)	5,228	254	682	4.85	8.18
year	22,980	1,204	2,163	5.23	4.17
1970 (1)	5,143	360	810	6.99	8.74
(2)	4,830	190	1,489	3.93	26.89
(3)	5,853	1,377	1,483	23.52	1.81
(4)	6,370	1,770	1,744	27.78	− .40
year	22,196	3,697	5,526	16.65	8.24
1971 (1)	7,579	2,315	1,145	30.54	− 15.43
(2)	7,808	1,523	1,550	19.50	.34
(3)	8,831	2,118	1,402	23.98	− 8.10
(4)	8,790	2,295	2,386	26.10	1.03
year	33,008	8,251	6,483	24.99	− 5.35
TOTAL 1969-71	78,184	13,152	14,172	16.82	1.30

[a] Including both single and multifamily housing starts.

[b] Includes subsidized housing programs of HUD (FHA), USDA, and VA but excludes public housing. The number of subsidized housing starts are converted to current dollars by multiplying annual starts by median unit value for each year.

Source: John H. Kalchbrenner, *Summary of the Current Financial Intermediary, Mortgage, and Housing Sectors of the SSRC-MIT-PENN-ECONOMETRIC MODEL,* material presented at the Housing Model Conference, Federal Home Loan Bank Board, Washington, D. C., March 5, 1971.

This analysis of possible output effects of housing subsidies is not intended to suggest that the elasticity of housing supply with respect to subsidy programs is generally high. It may be high during times of excess industry capacity such as the 1969-71 period. During periods of full employment in the housing industry, however, the subsidy programs may serve to reallocate resources within the industry, and at the same time bid up prices of factor inputs in the construction process. In such periods, cuts in the subsidy programs might have little effect on total production and would slow inflationary tendencies.

It is impossible to compare the new equilibrium value of output brought about by housing subsidies for lower-income households with the equilibrium value of output in the absence of the subsidies. Whether the new equilibrium is "better" depends upon the level of resource efficiency of the original equilibrium. Generally, if growth in the housing stock falls short of population growth, housing subsidies may be helpful. However, over the 1950-70 period, decennial census data indicate that the stock, both inside and outside metropolitan areas, increased at a substantially faster rate than population.

Despite the fact that the size of the average household declined from 3.1 to 2.7 persons from 1950 to 1970, and the number of households increased even faster than population, housing construction provided 1.5 new residences for each new household formed. Crowded housing, defined in terms of more than one person per room, dropped from 16 to 7 percent of the total stock between 1950 and 1970. The proportion of dilapidated housing fell from 10 to 5 percent of the total from 1950 to 1960 and was not counted in 1970. This occurred despite the fact that government programs were responsible for destroying about as much housing as they built during this period. The net improvement in the housing stock from 1950 to 1970, both in number and in quality, came from activity in the private sector.

These data indicate that the encouragement of new housing production by means of subsidy programs may foster less efficient long-run equilibrium. The issue does not turn on whether there is a housing problem for lower-income households, but rather on whether efforts to solve it should rely on new construction or on provision of better housing services from the existing housing stock. It may be far less costly and more efficient to give low-income households the funds to buy whatever housing services they wish, whether from existing or newly constructed stock, than to subsidize construction intended specifically for their occupancy.

The Cost of Housing Subsidies

Budgetary expenditures by the federal government for all subsidies associated with the Section 235 and 236 programs cannot be added up neatly. First, the interest rate and tax subsidies flow over a number of years, but subsidy payments under the GNMA-FNMA Tandem Plan are made in one lump sum (to absorb discounts when the permanent mortgage is issued). Second, payments of interest rate subsidies may vary over time according to changes in the levels of homeowner and tenant incomes and, in the case of multifamily rental housing, of operating costs. Third, tax losses are a function of investors' income tax brackets and of their decisions regarding when to sell equity interests in low-income housing and whether to roll over the sales proceeds into the same kind of project.

Table 6

ESTIMATED FUTURE BUDGET EXPENDITURES FOR INTEREST RATE CASH SUBSIDIES CONTRACTED, FISCAL YEARS 1969-73 [a]

Item	Section 235	Section 236
Contract authority (thousands)	$ 665,000	$ 675,000
Number of units supported	710,300	725,700
Maximum years commitment	30	40
Estimated years subsidy paid	11-14	19-25
Maximum contractual payments (thousands)	$19,950,000	$27,000,000
Estimated contractual payments (thousands)	$ 4,961,422	$10,840,991 [b]

[a] This table provides estimates in current dollars for the maximum and expected level of the interest rate cash subsidies that the federal government has contracted to pay over the life of mortgages issued to finance subsidized housing produced in the 1969-73 period. Estimated contractual payments are considerably lower than maximum contractual payments because subsidy payments are based for all practical purposes on the difference between fixed monthly mortgage payments (or equivalent "market rents") amortized at market interest rates and fixed proportions of homeowner or tenant income. Subsidy payments thus will decline as personal incomes rise. In the case of rental units, however, HUD-authorized increases in rents to cover higher operating expenses will retard the abatement of subsidy payments.

[b] These payments include the federal government's share of the capitalized value of wage subsidies in those instances when Section 236 projects are built by labor receiving wages higher than market rates on account of distortions in "prevailing wage determinations."

Source: U.S. Congress, House of Representatives, Subcommittee on HUD-Space-Science-Veterans, *Hearings on HUD-Space-Science-Veterans Appropriations for 1973,* part 3, 92nd Congress, 2nd session, pp. 109-16.

The analysis that follows attempts first to quantify in constant dollars the flow of subsidy payments over future time periods, and then to derive the present value of these flows. Table 6 displays estimates prepared by HUD for the cost over time of the interest subsidies contracted by the federal government for Section 235 and 236 housing during the fiscal years 1969-73. Estimated subsidy payments are substantially lower and run for a shorter time than maximum contracted obligations for reasons amplified in the footnote to the table. Total payments are estimated at $16 billion in current dollars spread over the period 1969-92.

The cost of the special assistance operations of GNMA under the Tandem Plan over the same period, in connection with the absorption of discount points on permanent mortgages issued under the Section 235 and 236 programs, is estimated at $100 million. Not all Section 235 and 236 mortgages made during the period, however, passed through the Tandem Plan.

The cost of tax subsidies provided to investors in low-income multifamily rental housing (foregone tax receipts to the U.S. Treasury) are provided in Table 7. These calculations are based on Schechter's estimates, and assume specific investor decisions regarding the time to sell equities in Section 236 projects and the share to be reinvested in other such equities (see above). On this basis, tax losses to the U.S. Treasury for Section 236 housing authorized in fiscal years 1969-73 amount to some $85 million in current dollars spread over 1969-83. These estimates do not include the benefits generated by accelerated depreciation because this privilege is available to investors in all new residential multifamily units.

The present value of the subsidies estimated above is shown in Table 8. This adjustment compensates for the fact that a dollar payable at some future date is not worth as much as a dollar paid out today. Moreover, since the various subsidies in the Section 235 and 236 programs do not have payment schedules of equal lengths, aggregated current dollar figures cannot be used to assess their current budgetary impact. A discount rate of 8 percent has been employed because it approximates the cost of money on private markets for guaranteed loans.

The figures indicate that the present value of the budgetary impact of future subsidy payments committed by HUD in fiscal years 1969-73 (the figure for 1973 is an estimate) is in the range of $8 billion. This figure is an estimate of the transfer cost imposed on the economy: it reflects a shift in real resources from some members of society to others rather than an increase in claims on real re-

Table 7
ESTIMATED TAX LOSSES GENERATED BY SECTION 236 HOUSING CONTRACTED IN FISCAL YEARS 1969-73

Item in Calculation	$ Millions
1. Estimated FHA-insured loans to limited distribution sponsors [a]	7,663
2. Equivalent replacement cost (111.11% of line 1)	8,514
3. Equity investment (10% of line 2)	851
4. Tax losses	85.0
Recapture provisions (up to 1979-83) [b]	(34.0)
Roll-over provisions (up to 1973-77) [c]	(51.0)

[a] Estimated on the basis of 725,700 units with an average mortgage of $16,500 per unit; limited-distribution sponsors account for 64 percent of total mortgagors.

[b] Assumes property is sold at original cost at the end of 10 years when all proceeds representing depreciated book value in excess of straight-line depreciation are taxed at the capital gains rate rather than "recaptured" at ordinary income tax rates. The value of this tax preference is estimated at 0.4 percent on equity investment annually over a 10-year period.

[c] Assume 25 percent of all projects are sold by investors (limited-partnership entities) to tenants or a cooperative or other nonprofit organization of the tenants and proceeds reinvested in other Section 236 projects as a means of indefinitely deferring capital gains taxes and the recapture of sales proceeds representing excess depreciation. The value of this tax preference is estimated at 6 percent on equity investment annually over a four-year period.

Source: Table 6; estimated rates of returns to investors from tax benefits are from Henry B. Schechter, *Federally Subsidized Housing Program Benefits* (Washington, D. C.: Library of Congress, Congressional Research Service, 1971).

Table 8
ESTIMATED PRESENT VALUE OF SUBSIDY PAYMENTS CONTRACTED IN FISCAL YEARS 1969-73 [a]
($ millions)

Item	Section 235	Section 236	Total
Interest rate cash subsidy (estimated contractual payments)	2,819	4,862	7,681
Absorption of discount points (Tandem Plan)	50	50	100
Tax Subsidies			
Recapture provisions	NA	25	25
Roll-over provisions	NA	46	46
Total present value	2,869	4,943	7,812

[a] All data discounted to present value at an 8 percent rate on a straight-line basis over maximum number of years estimated that subsidy payments will be made.

Source: Tables 6 and 7; Tandem Plan data obtained from HUD.

sources, and it serves as a measure of the current budgetary impact of commitments already entered into by the federal government. The figures also indicate that, on the basis of their present value, the total cost of subsidy payments for housing produced under the Section 235 and 236 programs during 1969-73 (again, including an estimate for 1973) amounts to $5,440 per unit. This amount includes the cost of subsidies provided specifically to consumers, producers, and production factors in the low-income housing market, but not the tax benefits available to residential housing markets generally.

V. EVALUATION AND CONCLUSIONS

This study of the subsidized housing programs conducted under Sections 235 and 236 has yielded the following results.

Evaluation

First, a review of the legislative history of housing subsidy programs for lower-income households suggests that the Congress has not invoked an *economic* justification for the use of subsidies as a tool of economic policy. No attempt has been made either to link subsidies directly with specific shortcomings of the marketplace, such as imperfect competition or externalities, or systematically to redistribute income within the economy. Rather, the avowed intent of the Congress has been to achieve quite general objectives—to increase employment, encourage new housing production, and make decent housing available to lower-income households.

The result has been that the programs have afforded benefits, but not exclusively to those in the lowest income category. These are legitimate goals, but it is not clear that subsidies are the best way to reach them. Moreover, while some benefits are generally perceived, little attention seems to have been paid to whether the benefits of these programs are worth their costs.

Second, the various subsidy schemes appear to have benefitted some low-income consumers of housing. In this sense they have been relatively effective in achieving the broad intent established by the Congress. This is true even though they may be unfair in their very uneven impact. Moreover, there have been many instances where purchasers of rehabilitated housing under the Section 235 program have been exploited by real estate operators. The mechanics of the program lead to fraudulent practices. Nevertheless, over the 1969-72 period, there are clear indications that, on a nationwide basis, the Section 235 and 236 subsidy programs reduced the price of housing to qualifying low-income households.

Also, they helped stimulate a higher level of housing production, at least in 1969-70, than would have been forthcoming otherwise. This was a period of substantial excess capacity in the housing industry. Consequently, the industry-wide price impact of housing subsidies and the diversion of resources from the construction of nonsubsidized housing were relatively insignificant. Whether these subsidy programs would appreciably increase the amount of construction during periods of full capacity utilization is less certain. In such periods, the industry-wide price impacts would undoubtedly be larger and favorable output effects smaller than in 1969-70. Curtailment of the subsidy programs in periods of full employment appears advisable.

Third, the Davis-Bacon Act is clearly an anomaly. The way in which it is administered supports a cartel for workers constructing housing for low-income households. The result has been a diversion of the subsidy nominally aimed at reducing the price of housing for the poor into the pockets of construction workers.

Fourth, to date, the Section 235 and 236 subsidy programs have been expensive, but probably not as expensive as some critics suggest. A best estimate would place the present value for subsidy payments associated with these programs contracted over fiscal years 1969-73 at about $8 billion, or about $5,400 per unit.

Fifth, no clear evidence confirms that the allocation of federal budgetary resources to finance housing construction subsidy programs, as opposed to other alternatives for achieving the goals of national housing policy, yields the highest return on public dollars invested. It is difficult to compare directly the new equilibrium value of output in the economy brought about by the housing subsidies with the equilibrium value in their absence. Considering that private housing starts exceeded population growth by a wide margin during the 1950-70 period, the return on public dollars invested in the subsidy programs may not be high. This is not to suggest that there is no housing problem, but to indicate that emphasis should be placed on increasing the availability of housing services generally to lower-income households rather than on attempts specifically to increase the supply of new low-cost units.

Sixth, the housing problem no longer concerns the incidence of substandard housing but the high cost of all housing. In the last two decades, substandard housing has diminished markedly as a proportion of the total stock, primarily as a consequence of private sector activities. Therefore, continuing programs of subsidies focused on new construction have little justification. However, with 15 percent of the poor in central cities and 21 percent of the poor in other urban areas still in substandard housing, there may be a justification for a demand-augmenting type of subsidy.

Ironically, the construction subsidy programs themselves constitute a reason for their own discontinuance, for it is the high cost of housing that is the current problem, and the programs are one of the factors driving up the cost. To the extent that subsidies are obtainable only by moving into newly constructed housing, they have led to the abandonment of sound structures, and thus, through the removal of stock that otherwise could have been maintained, driven up the cost of housing.

Finally, insofar as the present housing subsidy programs are linked to new construction, they spur the building of homes but not their maintenance. Subsidized tenants are locked into subsidized units. If maintenance is inadequate, they can complain but in most cases they cannot move out without losing their subsidy. Without the incentive to maintain subsidized housing, owners and tenants allow it to deteriorate more rapidly. As a consequence, construction subsidies are inefficient as means of adding to the long-run supply of housing. The effectiveness of subsidies has been sacrificed on the altar of new housing starts, as one observer has remarked.

Conclusions

What, then, are the alternatives? First and foremost, national housing policy should aim at eliminating existing impediments to the proper functioning of the housing markets. Interest rate ceilings on HUD-insured mortgages, restrictive building codes, "prevailing wage determinations" under the Davis-Bacon Act, and bottlenecks imposed on the training of construction manpower are examples of obstacles whose removal could be the focus of an effective policy.

Second, national housing policy should be concerned not only with increasing the supply of decent housing at proper locations through new construction but also with assuring that sufficient demand exists to permit the maintenance of the existing stock from which housing services flow. The inability of many households to secure adequate housing services is the result of poverty. This problem might best be attacked through demand-augmenting subsidies, provided by an income maintenance program or housing allowance.

The main advantages of the income maintenance and housing allowance approaches over the present subsidy programs is that they permit the recipients more choice in the use of funds, may be more efficient and less liable to fraud, and are more equitable. Under these alternatives, *all* lower-income households would have equal access to housing subsidies, while the present subsidy programs operate on a first-come, first-served basis for eligible households.

Moreover, demand-augmenting subsidies generally assist recipients in obtaining used as well as new housing. The present supply-augmenting programs change the relative prices of used and new housing and thereby push the poor toward new units, which afford a level of housing services that may be in excess of their needs. The poor might well prefer less expensive used housing to a new Section 236 unit if they could purchase other goods with the money saved.

Both types of subsidies have adverse price effects and therefore impose costs on the general public aside from the tax burden required to finance the subsidies. By increasing demand, housing allowances drive up the price of housing, whose supply can be expanded over time only by drawing resources away from other sectors of the economy. Likewise, the present subsidy programs increase the supply of housing by attracting factors of production at higher prices into the housing industry from other sectors, thereby increasing the price of housing services. In this sense, the economic consequences of the two forms of subsidy are identical. From an equity viewpoint, however, demand-augmenting subsidies are clearly preferable.

On the grounds of efficiency, demand-augmenting subsidies may also have the advantage. For any desired level of housing stock, fewer economic resources may be required to maintain and rehabilitate *existing* housing than to build *new* housing that furnishes comparable flows of housing services. By reducing the rate of deterioration, abandonment, and demolition of existing units, demand-type subsidies may achieve a more efficient use of resources in the housing industry. This is an important consideration because the number of existing housing units destroyed annually in the United States rivals the number of new subsidized housing starts. Some of the destruction that stems from abandonment may be a direct consequence of the subsidy program that attracts tenants from existing units to new ones that enjoy the subsidy.

Another advantage of housing allowances over interest rate subsidies is their portability. If tenants move from a subsidized unit, they lose their subsidy, but they could take their allowances with them. Furthermore, because tenants who benefit from a subsidy cannot use it to shop for existing housing, their landlords do not have to worry about competing to retain tenants and are not encouraged to keep subsidized projects livable. As a consequence, maintenance is often inadequate and tenants are embittered. Recent hearings in the House of Representatives on subsidized projects uncovered widespread mismanagement (as well as evidence of outright fraud in the development and sale of housing under the program).[1]

Allowances or rental certificates could stretch the government's subsidy dollar. Current programs of construction (interest) subsidies in New York cost $3,500 to $5,000 a year per assisted family. It has been estimated that an allowance system could provide equivalent housing in used structures for $1,500.

As Richard Muth has pointed out:

> Under the rental certificate [housing allowance] program . . . the enhanced rental expenditures of lower income families would provide producers of housing with the means for producing additional housing. They would be permitted to provide it in the cheapest way they could. . . .
> Dwelling units would not have to be newly constructed or rehabilitated in set ways in order to be eligible for the program. If a producer could persuade participating families to spend their rent certificate on one of his dwellings by repairing broken windows and repainting rather than by installing new kitchens, he would be allowed to do so. . . . The program would thus provide private incentives to improve the slums rather than requiring that slum housing be demolished.[2]

A comparison of the impact that demand- and supply-augmenting subsidies would have on principal economic variables is sketched in Table 9. The symmetry of the two subsidy forms can be studied by comparing columns (1) and (2). The fundamental advantage of demand-augmenting subsidies stems from the expected favorable effect on industry-wide prices: fewer resources are required to maintain a given flow of housing services that is supplied by upgrading and maintaining existing dwellings rather than building new ones.

On balance, the analysis in this study suggests that while HUD's principal programs of housing subsidies have not been as inefficient and costly as some critics argue, there is good reason (especially as the economy reaches capacity utilization of its resources) to give serious consideration to curtailing the Section 235-236 programs and supplementing or replacing them with housing allowances. A strong argument can be made that allowances are more equitable than subsidies. They are, furthermore, more efficient and they minimize the decay and abandonment of city centers that construction subsidies have perversely encouraged.

Table 9

IMPACT OF DEMAND- AND SUPPLY-AUGMENTING HOUSING SUBSIDIES ON PRINCIPAL ECONOMIC VARIABLES
Benefits (+)/Costs (−)

Item	Demand-Augmenting Subsidies	Supply-Augmenting Subsidies
Rate of construction activity	+	+
Rate of abandonment	+ a	− b
Quality of stock	+	+
Price of housing services	+	+
Subsidized households	+	+
Nonsubsidized renter	−	−
Nonsubsidized homeowners	+	−
Construction industry	+	+
Owners of standard rental housing	+	−

a Poor abandon substandard housing in favor of either better used or new housing and substandard housing is improved where it is efficient to do so.

b Poor abandon substandard and standard housing in favor of subsidized new units and incentives to upgrade substandard sound structures diminish.

NOTES

NOTES TO SECTION I

[1] Comptroller General of the United States, *Opportunity to Improve Allocation of Program Funds to Better Meet the National Housing Goal,* report transmitted to Congress, October 2, 1970, p. 2.

The Comptroller General's report also concluded: "HUD records show that, from 1949 through June 30, 1968, 552,896 dwelling units for low- and moderate-income families had been constructed nationwide under all HUD programs.... This number ... is only about 113,000 in excess of the 439,626 units that had been demolished under the urban renewal program as of June 30, 1968, and does not take into consideration the many thousands of demolitions resulting from other HUD programs (such as public housing) and other federal programs (such as the federal highway program) and activities carried out by the communities (such as code enforcement and street and school construction." (p. 19)

[2] National Commission on Urban Problems, *Building the American City* (Washington, D. C.: U.S. Government Printing Office, 1968); President's Committee on Urban Housing, *A Decent Home* (Washington, D. C.: U.S. Government Printing Office, 1968).

[3] *Third Annual Report on National Housing Goals,* message from the President to Congress (Washington, D. C.: U.S. Government Printing Office, 1971), p. 22.

[4] U.S. Congress, House of Representatives, Hearings before the Committee on Banking and Currency, *Interim Report on HUD Investigation of Low and Moderate Income Housing Programs,* 92nd Congress, 1st session.

[5] The mortgage limits are $21,000 except for families of five or more buying a four-bedroom house, in which case the limit is $24,000.

[6] Statement by Philip C. Jackson, Jr., president, Mortgage Bankers Association, as reported in National Association of Home Builders, *Journal of Homebuilding,* June 1972, p. 14; see also "Program Critics are Ignoring Substantial Public Benefits," *Journal of Homebuilding,* June 1972, pp. 26-30; Anthony Downs, *Federal Housing Subsidies: Their Nature and Effectiveness and What We Should Do About Them,* prepared for the National Association of Home Builders, National Association of Mutual Savings Banks, and United States Savings and Loan League, October 1972.

NOTES TO SECTION II

[1] For a description of HUD's mandate, see U.S. Congress, House of Representatives, Subcommittee on HUD-Space-Science-Veterans, *Hearings on HUD-Space-Science-Veterans Appropriations for 1973,* part 3, 92nd Congress, 2nd session, pp. 81-91; Donald D. Kummerfeld, "The Housing Subsidy System," *Papers Submitted to Subcommittee on Housing Panels,* U.S. Congress, House of Representatives, Committee on Banking and Currency, 92nd Congress, 1st session, pp. 451-54.

[2] Construction is only the first step in providing housing services. For a discussion of the need to link subsidies directly to services, see Morton L. Isler, "The Goals of Housing Subsidy Programs," in *Papers Submitted to Subcommittee on Housing Panels,* pp. 415-36. Congress has authorized operating subsidies for public housing in the Brooke amendment, which stipulates that federal funds can be used to cover operating deficits of public housing projects.

³ For a detailed discussion of the legislative history of U.S. housing programs, see Henry B. Schechter, *Federal Housing Subsidy Programs* (Washington, D.C.: Library of Congress, Congressional Research Service, 1971). Also, see *Housing and Urban Development Bills* (Washington, D. C.: American Enterprise Institute, 1968).

⁴ The FHA residential mortgage program is self-financing in that developers' fees and homeowners' insurance premiums cover the costs of mortgage default.

⁵ Some neighborhoods evidently have been worsened by federal housing programs. The Pruitt-Igoe project in St. Louis, the Cabrini project in Chicago, and the Roger Williams project in Providence all have very high vacancy ratios because eligible families are fearful of living in them. Daniel N. Wilner et al., *The Housing Environment and Family Life* (Baltimore: Johns Hopkins Press, 1962), suggests that improved housing as such has little effect on the health or social adjustment of tenants.

⁶ The Comptroller General of the United States reported in 1970 that in six projects his office examined in detail, a very large proportion of the residents had been housed in housing of standard quality before moving into the projects. See *Opportunity to Improve Allocation of Program Funds.*

⁷ See John J. Agria, *College Housing: A Critique of the Federal College Housing Loan Program* (Washington, D. C.: American Enterprise Institute, 1972).

⁸ Monroe W. Kamin, "Direct Payments for Housing the Poor," *Wall Street Journal,* January 10, 1972, p. 8.

⁹ For a detailed description, see Schechter, *Federal Housing Subsidy Programs.*

¹⁰ A detailed discussion of the public housing and urban renewal programs may be found in Richard F. Muth, *Public Housing: An Economic Evaluation* (Washington, D. C.: American Enterprise Institute, 1973), and John C. Weicher, *Urban Renewal: National Program for Local Problems* (Washington, D. C.: American Enterprise Institute, 1973).

¹¹ This discussion does not include subsidies in the form of tax preferences provided under Section 167/K of the IRS Code. This section refers to the five-year depreciation write-off period available to investors in rental rehabilitated low-income housing. Rehabilitated housing production has amounted to a relatively small share of total subsidized housing production.

¹² See in particular, U.S. Congress, Joint Economic Committee, *The Economics of Federal Subsidy Programs,* 92nd Congress, 1st session, pp. 41-42.

¹³ In a study of the Davis-Bacon Act, John P. Gould found that "prevailing wage determinations" were usually above market wages when a significant share of the local labor force was unionized. In such cases, the Department of Labor tended to use labor union wage scales exclusively for measurement purposes rather than to include nonunion wage scales. John P. Gould, *Davis-Bacon Act: The Economics of Prevailing Wage Laws* (Washington, D. C.: American Enterprise Institute, 1971); see also, Comptroller General of the United States, report to the Congress, *Need for Improved Administration of the Davis-Bacon Act Noted Over a Decade of General Accounting Office Reviews* (Washington, D. C.: General Accounting Office, 1971).

¹⁴ Contractors who work primarily on privately financed construction often avoid federally sponsored construction because the "prevailing wage determinations" create two wage scales for each skill level and job category.

NOTES TO SECTION III

¹ U.S. Congress, Joint Economic Committee, *The Economics of Federal Subsidy Programs,* 92nd Congress, 1st session, pp. 1-6; see also, Joint Economic Committee, *Subsidy and Subsidy-Effect Programs of the U.S. Government,* 89th

Congress, 1st session. The discussion of subsidies in this section relies heavily on these sources. For a discussion of subsidies available to persons of all income levels in the form of mortgage interest and property tax deductions, see Henry Aaron, "Income Taxes and Housing," *American Economic Review*, vol. 60, no. 5 (December 1970), pp. 789-806.

[2] Commission on Mortgage Interest Rates, *Report to the President of the United States and to the Congress* (Washington, D. C.: U.S. Government Printing Office, 1969). Another view is that the interest rate elasticity of housing demand is primarily responsible for the reduction of funds flowing into mortgage markets when interest rates rise.

[3] Lester C. Thurow, "Goals of a Housing Program," in *Papers Submitted to Subcommittee on Housing Panels*, U.S. Congress, House of Representatives, Committee on Banking and Currency, 92nd Congress, 1st session, pp. 438-39.

[4] Muth, *Public Housing*, pp. 22-30.

[5] Dan Larkins, *$300 Billion in Loans* (Washington, D. C.: American Enterprise Institute, 1972), p. 50.

[6] In the Housing Act of 1970, Congress authorized an experiment in housing allowances to see if in fact they have a greater price incidence than output effect. A recent study suggests that such demand subsidies might be dissipated in rent increases rather than leading to more housing services. See Frank De Leeuw and N. F. Ekanem, "The Supply of Rental Housing," *American Economic Review*, vol. 61, no. 5 (December 1971), pp. 806-17.

[7] Richard F. Muth, *Cities and Housing* (Chicago: University of Chicago Press, 1969), pp. 278-79.

NOTES TO SECTION IV

[1] William B. Ross, "A Proposed Methodology for Comparing Federally Assisted Housing Programs," *American Economic Review*, vol. 57, no. 2 (May 1967), pp. 91-100. Henry B. Schechter, *Federally Subsidized Housing Program Benefits* (Washington, D.C.: Library of Congress, Congressional Research Service, 1971), p. 3.

[2] Schechter, *Federally Subsidized Housing Program Benefits*, pp. 12-23 and 26-39. The Section 207 program provides HUD mortgage insurance for multifamily housing generally having larger units and more amenities than Section 236 housing.

[3] The mortgage terms are comparable on Section 207 and 236 projects and the median mortgage per unit is about the same ($15,172 for Section 207 and $14,975 for Section 236 in 1970), although Section 207 units are larger in size and include more amenities, such as elevators. The higher median market rent for Section 207 units (the difference is $13) may be explained largely by the higher equity investment requirements and operating and maintenance expenses as well as by the larger size and additional amenities. Ibid.

[4] Ibid., p. 11; see also Mortgage Bankers Association of America, *Quarterly Economic Report*, October 1970.

[5] Schechter, *Federally Subsidized Housing Program Benefits*; Arthur Andersen & Co., "Tax Sheltered Investments" (Chicago, 1970), subject file AA 3040, item 1, pp. 13-15.

[6] For a discussion of investor behavior in multifamily housing, see report by Touche Ross & Co. to HUD, "Study of Tax Concessions in Multifamily Housing Investments," in *Hearings on HUD-Space-Science-Veterans Appropriations for 1973*, pp. 1391-1408.

[7] Comptroller General of the United States, *Need for Improved Administration of Davis-Bacon Act*, p. 9.

[8] John H. Kalchbrenner, *Summary of the Current Financial Intermediary, Mortgage, and Housing Sectors of the SSRC-MIT-PENN-ECONOMETRIC Model,* material presented at the Housing Model Conference, Federal Home Loan Bank Board, Washington, D. C., March 5, 1971.

NOTES TO SECTION V

[1] See U.S. Congress, House Committee on Banking and Currency, *Interim Report on HUD Investigation of Low and Moderate Income Housing Programs;* "General Statement of Secretary Romney" in *Hearings on HUD-SPACE-SCIENCE-VETERANS Appropriations for 1973,* part 3, pp. 32-33; and U.S. Department of Housing and Urban Development, Office of Audit, *Audit Review of Section 235 Single Family Housing* (December 10, 1971) and *Report on Audit of Section 236 Multifamily Housing Program* (January 29, 1972).

[2] Muth, *Public Housing,* pp. 48-49.

Book design: Pat Taylor
Cover: The Philadelphia maze